T0114699

The Path
Walked On

JENNIFER MAE

BALBOA.PRESS
A DIVISION OF HAY HOUSE

Balboa Press books may be ordered through booksellers or by contacting:

Balboa Press
A Division of Hay House
1663 Liberty Drive
Bloomington, IN 47403
www.balboapress.com
844-682-1282

Print information available on the last page.

ISBN: 979-8-7652-2802-9 (sc)
ISBN: 979-8-7652-2803-6 (e)

Balboa Press rev. date: 10/12/2022

I dedicate this book to all empaths, sensitives and deep feelers

Contents

Shadows

Betwixt

Rays of Light

Introduction & Acknowledgments

I could not have put this poetry book together without many twisted steps taken on a hilly path. For a good part of my life, I have felt the depths of loneliness and not belonging. I have come to realize that I was never truly alone on that path. There were many teachers along the way. Some taught me lessons that have lurked in my shadows and turned my soul. Some were guides leading me to rays of light. Step by step I have arrived here. In sharing my poems, my desire is that you might recognize a feeling, or have a spark of light enter your heart.

I was guided to buy an audio book written by a medium. This book was so insightful and led me to a class she teaches on mediumship. But could I? The time and the cost wagged their tails in my face and screamed "No"! My husband encouragingly said, "Why not? If that is what you want to do, then we will figure it out." In that class, I learned many things, but the lasting effect it had on me, was to once and for all TRUST myself. Thank you to this generous medium, her life-changing class and to my loving husband.

Another outcome of the class I took was to be part of a medium circle. In that circle, we practiced our connections with spirit, but we also became friends, mentors and support for each other. A safe place to be our authentic selves. A friend from the circle recommended Hay House as a resource for books, courses and card decks. I found a writer's workshop there and this led to Balboa Press and self-publishing. Thank you to my much cherished medium circle.

Could I really do it? Could I publish my poems that have been sitting in a handwritten journal for almost thirty years? Again, my husband said, "why not?" Ok, here it goes, making my dreams come true and putting myself out into the world. Excuse me while I vomit for a minute. Just, kidding, well, not really. Something pushed way deep down in the depths of shadows makes a mess as it comes back up to breathe.

Thank you to my husband for his steadfast support and encouragement. Thank you to my two daughters for putting aside some playtime while I worked on my poems and book. Thank you to my mom and dad, sister and brother, nephews and niece, and best friends who all cheered me on. So much love to each and every one of you. And thank you to my spirit guides, loved ones in Heaven, and many Angels who have guided me, pushed me, and showed me that they had my back every step of the way.

Shadows

Violation

The First Touch
towering beside me
gangly
stench of Vodka stinging my nose
a vast field
a tremendous sky...

it slithers across the back of my neck
and hangs off my shoulder
it hits the extension of my heart
my flesh
which tingles and tries to retract
it comes at me again
but harder
"Stop"
dribbles off my lips
which are than forced on
my scream evaporates
absorbed by the dark creature

The Kiss
the power comes to me
face to face
it comes closer as my body trembles
i try and turn away
but the magnet pulls me in
without a choice
the poison slides across my face
and presses on my lips
the voice of my soul

No"
is not understood
not heard
perhaps it is heard
but only as a challenge
my conscious mind refuses to believe
the circumstances that are taking away
the vitality of my life

Shadows

<u>The Walk</u>
the field leads to a road
the cars pass by without a clue
of what this boy is doing to this girl

the hill we walk up is like
climbing the steepest staircase
while the boy probes about my maidenhood
i refuse to answer

i wanted to answer
to pretend that this
was a normal conversation

i ceased to exist
as i watched four people
struggling to the flagpole
the boys stumbled away
the girl saw escape

she felt relief and started to rush
back to the beginning to
undo all that didn't happen

"i love you"
echoed in the air and
in her mind

the misery was not even close to being over

<u>The Attack</u>
from behind
the two boys come
out of nowhere
one boy and my best friend
disappeared up ahead
i was left alone
i wish i was alone

hot breath stained my ear
numbness paralyzed my body
fear, intimidation, all of my dreams
sweat out of my pores
i was surrounded by a hole

Shadows

The Grab
the flesh that is shared only by love
was taken
his hands touched all that was
not his
he left his prints like toxic radiation
that would never heal
all was ruined

but she gathered up her strength
wobbled a few steps away
the grab held her back
for eternity

the wrist was clenched
and it disappeared
it was tugged on
yanked
pulled
and burned
that part no longer existed
but made me a prisoner
without hope
life was at an end

The Fall
i whispered refusals...
"if you wont tell me if you're chaste,
i'll have to find out for myself"

steps away
the wrist was grabbed
again
pressure on my chest
made my knees give out
i hit the cold earth
the weeds were as dry as a desert
the being flung on me
i see blackness

3

Shadows

<u>The Angel</u>
somehow
a power got me on my feet
the girl pushed the boy away
and stumbled towards the parking lot
every step was unrealistic
mind was spinning
car was there
with my best friend and her mom
sitting was safety

"what do i do?"
"don't tell"
she did not understand
i was all alone

disbelief of this violence set in
the process of forgetting was
just starting
but it never went away...

<u>Forgiving</u>
hate in my cavity
burned like undying fuel
my body was ripped apart
by this pain
i wanted revenge
for no one ever taught me how
to hate
before

yet this anger produced guilt
what right did i have
to judge him?
no one knows what it's like
to be the bad man
something must have happened
to him
to make him do
what he did to me

Shadows

this is what he learned
how could i
blame him?

i felt even worse for this anger
my worlds clashed
the banging was so loud
i needed escape
i can't let him continue to
hurt me

finally it came
peace
understanding
he is at fault
but i will not judge
i must move on
he is human
and so am i

Forgiveness...

Maple Avenue

i met him on the corner of the street
white t-shirt, blue jeans
fuzzy haze rising out of the sewers
cars honking in a rhythm of confusion
not a word was spoken
only a slight gaze

our feet led us to a diner
the door squeals open
bells jingle overhead
dingy linoleum resonates from his boots
the booth is lime green
the ceiling fan whips the dead air with tremendous force
as the seat glues itself to my skin

my hair falls in my face
the curls remind me of getting ready for dances
my nail polish shines from the dim light to the side
the table displays a ring of coffee
4 sparks of the lighter before a flame takes over
smoke rises above his face to touch the ceiling
ice moves, trying to melt, in my glass of water

he takes my hand with both of his
his eyes penetrate mine
his chest stretches his shirt while he breathes
i breathe in the faint scent of his cologne
an older man catches my glance as he exits the bathroom door
my love squeezes my hand
i let my eyes roam over his beauty

our bodies lean towards one another
i slowly close my eyes as my head tilts
his soft lips pressed against mine
his love flows over my mouth
my lips are pulled, then released
his eyes fall on my face
as his fingers linger on my cheek

Shadows

wheels screech to a stop on the hot pavement
bells jingle as a man in a suit enters
the man sits on a stool at the counter
the stool creeks as it turns
his dark eyes find us
the man approaches and stands at the end of the table
his jacket moves back to display a gun

a hand surrounds the handle
the gun raises from the holster
a strong finger presses the trigger
my love releases my hand
he falls against the back of the booth
head knocking against the wood
his hair falls in his face

his heart colors his white t-shirt red
while his skin loses color
my love's eyelids cover his vacant eyes
i look at the man in the suit
the man returns with his dark eyes
he slowly turns and strolls to the door
bells jingle overhead

The Store Window

cold air enters her lungs
she zips her coat up to her neck
the edge of her skirt dances on her thighs
heels echo on the deserted sidewalk
the street lamps buzz
the stop light continually blinks it's red glare
old newspapers whirl in the vacant road

a faint light falls on the ground from a window
she is drawn to this display of merchandise
worn red point shoes tug on her attention
it then shifts to a gold pocket watch hanging from a peg in the sidewall
an old unfamiliar magazine shows a picture of an extraterrestrial
a gold pearl ring lays on the carpeted windowsill
green plastic grapes sit in a wooden bowl

the breeze blows back her hair and skirt
she turns the corner and sees the fountain in the distance
water droplets catching the light of the lamp
spray fills the night air
dark gray statutes open their eyes and follow her
a light on the ground shines upwards
a dark figure stands solemnly in front of this light

the woman approaches the other
they stand regarding each other
two women, two strangers
the invisible wall between them
was felt as the cool air was felt
anger under the confusion
love under the anger
no comprehension
she left this woman when she was only a child

Six Million

Single drop of blood, bright red
lives on the cement
Reaching out to where it belonged
with its many tentacles

Single ash
lands in the dirt
Hot from the death flame
as screams linger in the stale air

Single smoke cloud
blackens the sky
Scattering bits throughout the world
to be utterly forgotten

Single teardrop
pushes away the grains of sand
Knowing the neglect
drying up as with all these souls

Stop

What?....no -

The wind that stopped blowing
The birds that stopped singing
The cars that stopped humming
The footsteps that faded
The smoke that dissipated
The tunnel that appeared

The eyes that did not close
The tears that absorbed the ground
The heart that was gripped
The knees that gave out
The body that did not stop shaking
The news that was so horrible to hear

The nonexistent world that runs around you
The lips that part and move to a smile
The laughter that echoes in this hollowness

Please stop and listen
There is no sound

Please stop and hear
The silence screams so loud

Please stop and help me get to my feet

Generations

Moving so quickly
But caught in their flight
Trapped on film
Each particle
frozen

Cold blasts zoom through
Siphoning my energy
Numbing my
arm

Making a connection of trust
Between two worlds
Yet they
followed...

The White Lady

The full moon shines through the black window
illuminating the white curtains and colorless walls
Like a spotlight on a woman lying in her long white nightgown
on light blue sheets
with her shiny blonde hair flowing over the metal bed frame

The lightning cracks and the thunder explodes
waking the woman in a startle
eyes bewildered
Her bare feet fall to the wooden floor

Flashes enlighten the room only to leave it dark
the crashes shake the window panes
Piercing the thunder is a cry from afar
The gold door knob on the dark oak door resists her pull

Straggling down the long hallway
she is being watched
as she approaches
the end and the beginning
of an old oak stairway that curves around
Someone is there

A body consumed in light
with piercing blue eyes and
a long brown braid
stands midway up the stairway
watching the women encroach

The power and knowledge carried by this being
paralyzes the woman
Yet the light creeps forward and
envelops her in a blanket of amity

She reaches out and feels
the urgency of this being to find her lost child
Walking each night
searching from one resting place
through the living
to another

Shadows

The woman watches powerless
as the lady in white disappears
in a burst of lightning
to continue her journey

Stopping traffic as the white lady walks
in chaos
with one destination that moves her

Waiting For A Diagnosis

Following the blue line
down the corridor
Plastic bags from construction
sway from her presence
Two women pass
one nods
the nun speaking a cordial hello
A man looks up from his chair
as she passes
Electric revolving doors
carry her to sunshine

The quiet car returns the lady home
The warm air is not noticed
neither are her steps
Thoughts are on telling her friends
as they talk, laugh, and play
from a very distant place

Waiting for the right time to call
trying to daydream this time away
Not knowing what to do with herself
she watches others until
the time that has surely come

yet only one minute has ticked by

The Crash

The smell of oil
choking my throat
Eyes weeping blackness
from the thick smoke
which moves swiftly
without sound

Shadows move within
searching in slow motion with
Desperation in their eyes
for any lingering life
within the charcoaled clothes

Quietness chills my bones
and tears burn my cheeks
Breath is extinguished...

The Icing

It reflects light with its dimensions
blanketing all
weighing down non-discriminately
the smoothness
paralyzes your fingertips

Gusts roar across the land
with its companion of dark clouds
the laden trees make their own music
as they twist in the air
A branch is thrown
to smack against the window
A scream invades the ear
the hair rises on your skin

Shattered pieces of ice and wood
cover the cold blacktop
reflecting that which was whole
strength uprooted.
laying across their path in finality
fear trembles in your limbs

A car is frozen
with a man and a woman
crushed into the plastic of the car
by the ice covered branch
desperation collapses your body

Renee

The sun shone down
through the branches
The woods quieted the air
around her

Her eyes widened as
the man of nothing appeared
and cast down a
shadow of fear

The strawberries
rolled down the slope
out of the basket

Her little brother
chased after those berries
and turned his head

As the hands brought
A rock down and
Renee closed her eyes

The brother sees her lying on the ground
and he kneels
to hold her hand

Dust In The Wind

surrounded by heat and sand
seven women and a man
hands and feet bound
await as doom approaches
Breath by Breath

trouble sits with them
fear clenches their hearts
the man in dull green stares at them
his dark shades and bullets
are like a photograph from a far away place
he speaks to them
they will be shot

the dirt blows around their feet
there is nothing to be done
the commander points his gun
and the one man hangs his head
realization sets in that
they are not ready to die

The Last Dance

Slowly
Step-by-step
Motion by motion
Word by word
i have come to experience you

Your delightfulness
Calls my heart
To wrap around to yours
And my lips to tell yours
Of my joy

Our lives just briefly joined
Are now parting into different worlds
Each heartbeat we get closer and closer
And each sunrise brings us further and further
Away

As you depart
My heart will unravel
And the threads will lead a trail to you
Soaked in tears

Cornflakes

The milk resting on the plastic tablecloth
checkered green and yellow
Granules of sugar
roughen the surface
The soggy cereal in the white bowl
that has been pushed away

The screen door that
has been exited
A woman sits in a beige wooden chair
that stares vacantly while her eyes
trickle her face with a salty burn

The shock that paralyzes her
swings away
The body that starts to tremble
shakes her spirit
vacillating in dead, humid air
taking a breath
only once a minute

The chair that was pushed back
scraping against the pale yellow tile
The four foot steps that lead her to
the pale wood cupboards

The clear glass that she placed in the sink
The cold water that overflowed

The pills that she stuffed in her mouth
The water that squeezed them down

The porch that awaits her
laying down on the white boards
A flower tips over
that soils the innocence...

The whistle that echoes down the walk
The feet anxious to surprise the woman
The ring that is fondled in his hands

Shadows

The face which terror took over
The stairs that hindered his aid
The clink as the ring falls to the wood

The woman that is held in his hands
The man that stares vacantly while his eyes
trickle his face with a salty burn
while he rocks back-and-forth

The scream of agony
that invades the sunny neighborhood

Open Hearts

Your guard is lifted and someone penetrates
To grab hold of your hidden heart
You let it go into their hands

A connection so deep
You sit with your mouth gaping open
In confused amazement

You could not feel a greater joy
Until you felt the worst pain

The door closed on the wounded scars
You were left hanging in the middle
Of nowhere

Something not so easily shared
Was handed back
On a broken platter

You grasp for understanding
While the pain deepens
And promise never to open again

Ancient Burnings

A million years ago
Was the last time i saw you
What will it be...

A glance, a stare
A nod, a handshake
A hug, a kiss
Or nothing?

i promised you a hug

The butterflies in my stomach
Rise to my heart
And colors my cheeks pink
Remembering what you saw in my soul

So close were we
That my imagination runs to fantasies
Of being with you
Yet knowing it will never be

i promised you a hug

Ponds

Four skips on the pond of the
perfect stone before
it sinks under the murky water

      i glance at her
      as the frogs speak to one another
      and the breeze blows through the cattails

my heart thrashes seeing her
trap herself
down in the pit of her existence

Messengers

The rumble begins
Waking us out of our slumber
The dark shadow creeps up
Manifesting a moving blanket
of sparrows

Which land leaving no more
Earth to live
Their cries increase
Drowning out all other
existence

The mass rises
To continue their pilgrimage
Of carrying the dying
to the dead

Trips

i was so determined to put each step
down firmly in what i have created
Alone to travel
with the world to satisfy my yearnings

Now i stop
My foot caught on an obstacle
i am frozen in the air
Not knowing whether to jump this hurdle
or to fall

The pull is strong
to reevaluate my being
and evaluate your meaning
The path is disappearing ahead of me
i don't know where to land

i chose a closure
now this trip tears little openings
Terror clenches, my eyes leak
What lays across my path?

The biggest struggle
is myself

Daily Survival

i struggle to stand up
my stomach churns
my eyes creek open

    to face the mirror

        my eyes have been punched
        my face drained of blood
        my lips hang down

            it is too easy to fall down

Fear

Hunkering on the edge of the bed
with hands on my knees
back curved
face drawn
jaw loose
eyes full

staring through the white light
invading the room

i stand at the door
the silence choking
my throat closed
gripping the stark pain

shutting down my motion

Unreciprocated

My chest is lacerated by
a careful incision
i do not even realize
i am exposed

My heart is removed
instead of being guarded
and plunges
to the sidewalk

There it sits as many pass by

Staring into its pulse
with your foot pressing down
it cannot beat
it cannot breathe

Finally rupturing
over the gray emptiness
ground into the cement
it can never reform

No longer a part of the world
numb and destroyed
with no where to go

Sacrifice

i LOST you before i knew you
        i let you fall
            after you tumbled into my palm
                        never to be nurtured

                        my life would have turned
                another direction
        altering all i aspired to have

    giving that away
            would have been easy

            but i LOST you

Endings

i hold a tissue

       where once was your hand

my arms encircle space

       where once was your body

i look in the frame

       where once was your picture

my gaze searches the blank walls

       where once were your writings

Scripts

Rushing

    searching

        desperate

           to find

              a way to escape

                    the ups and downs

                        of your real-life

                              drama

Discovering

    i did not

        fit

           the role

              you assigned

                    me

Relentless

Your eyes avert themselves from
my existence
Your words strike at me
in third person
You stride right through me
pretending my body didn't fill that space

Angel turned demon
in your thoughts
Evil i must be

Losing all my beauty and goodness
as i fell
off your pedestal

i invite you to look deeper

or would you just
fall on your knees
and worship
again

No Where

crying so loud but i'm the only one who hears
now where am i supposed to go from here
laying down seems to take up my life
thinking about what it'd be like to be your wife

i'm listening to the rain roll down
searching for a place in this small town
no where seems like a good fit
i'm going to have to leave in just a bit

why can't i find somewhere to slow down
i change my mind before i even turn around
these restless feet have me dancing 'cross the nation
in a little while you'll see me waving from the station

this sweet love has me singing to the heavens
for strength not to leave you only my reflections

the little one that is growing inside
needs to know that i wont run and hide
it wants a daddy to answer their questions
and not a void to encourage their inquisition

Walk Like A Man

To be able

to walk down my street
go anywhere alone
with no fear
of being blamed for existing
because some man decided
to attack me

To be able

to be looked at as a person
and not as some object
that is judged
ugly or pretty

One wish

of being me
with no body attached
to be controlled

Hands

Almost in prayer
        THEY come towards me

Yet encircle my neck
        instead of each other

                heat pouring out of your eyes
                anger seeping out of your pores

      i do not believe THEY are real
      as my vision fades and i fall

i cough myself awake and
        realize what THEY could do

Puppet Master

Slowly she weaved the strings

    one by one attached them to my

        hands and feet

           and they grew into

                my brain and heart

                    two people couldn't be closer

Until i resisted the pull

    unearthed that she was creating a

        mold for only her and

           did not like who i was at all

i cut the strings to be free

    to be vivacious in my own being

           But then the master disappeared

Unwelcome

What do i do
when your face floats by
pointing in the direction
averted from me

while your eyes
seep through
the back of your head
assaulting my presence

Misplaced

Giving all i can
in support
and waiting
until i don't know
where i am
anymore
and still
no love
returns

Art

The words echoed through the
rays of sunlight engulfing
my cheek

i could feel your gaze
lovingly embracing the
draped in black crowd below

the peace of closure that
should have come
did not arrive
to the soft ground beneath
my feet

thinking of the last touch
of your hand and the
earnest pleading
that streamed from your eyes

Shadows

Heartbreak

The ache so deep

it's roots reach down

and strangle

my heart

Heaviness lulls

inside

where can i go

How do i survive

Addiction

i say goodbye
Tears gushing from my heart
falling to the ground in small
circles surrounding my feet
with small extensions reaching out
to grab one another
trying to make whole
Soaking the cotton fibers of
your sleeve as i never want to
let go

You pull away harshly and the
void slams my body so
forcefully that
i cannot breathe

The ache is heavy and i can
barely stand straight
Panic sets in
i feel
i need
to explode or die
of the pain
i shake and sob trying to
force the pain away
but that one will never leave

Thoughts pound
relentless
Blocking any rational ideas
It will not stop and i cannot bear to
stand another moment like this

Cries of Mother Earth

Tear
  Rip
    Crash
      Bang
        Pour

           Stillness
           Dead Calm
           Quiet
           Placidity

                Chaos
                  Yelling
                    Screaming
                  Sirens

                    Despair

Agony

Staring blankly
at a screen of words
nothing makes sense
trying to piece together
the information to
make it coherent

Pain stabs the heart
heavy
pulling
downward
into an abyss
pounding fast
shakes the body

Forearms frozen
tight
strand by strand of muscle
intertwining into an
inescapable knot
hands become useless
claws

Just breathe

It wont stop

Prying fingers open
attempting to soften

But alas
the unforgiven agony
persists

Knocking

Sulfur stinging my nose
heavy wet cough escapes my mouth
crusty gunk pulls apart as I open my eyes
whining enters my ears
the white sheets stick to my hand
as I try to pull away and lift my head

Bang
a rock slams against the inside of my skull

The floor finds my feet
which I shuffle little by little
towards the door

Air rushes into my lungs
and into the hole in
my head

Help me

Fissures

A shell
of smooth blush porcelain

A crack here
running vertically
jagged
dark
Cracks there...
everywhere

O
h
G
o
d
N
o

shaking
trembling
sharp,
painful breaths
sobbing
screaming
whirling
weakness
collapse

another
fissure
appears

Tsunami

A crack here
          a crack there
                    spreading
                              connecting
                                   small
                                        but growing
                                                  widening
                                                            joining
                                                  darkness
                                        rising up
                              through the
                                             c
                                             r
                                             a
                                             c
                                             k
                                             s

                              pushing

                              congealing

                              forming

                         together
                    as one
          massive
w
a
v
e

          it
                    crashes
                              down...

Deep

i open my eyes
Where am i?
How did i get here?

i thought i was on top of the hill
on a strong path

but here i am
underneath this
heaviness
overwhelm
despair

i can't even look up
turn my head
or even want
to grab a bubble in the distant murkiness

just here
weighed down
confused
condemning
desolate

Hoarse

Screaming so loud
but you do not hear
i look up at you to take this pain away

You look down on me confused
at a crossroads of decision
to ignore that which is not understood
or to embrace the unknown and provide comfort
teaching
processing
releasing

back is turned as tears stream down the face

Maybe i can scream louder
rage
pierce the brain like an ice pick
slicing through
make you feel what i am feeling

Then you would know how deeply i
hurt
feel exposed

But my scream cannot sustain
and it fades
quietly into life
never to be heard from again

Tongue Bitten

i bite my tongue
100 times a day

afraid to speak
be true
from my point of view

you say things
freely
that are
wrong
that cast a dimness
over me

i want to stand up
clear the air
shake off
the shroud

as blood
trickles
out of the corners of
my mouth

my tongue so
grated
it doesn't know
how to work

Decimated

You are
>> Spent
>> Starving
>> Malnourished
>> LOST

You make
>> No sense
Leaving others to decipher

You embrace
>> Fear
>> Anger
>> Hate
>> Hopelessness

You bathe in
>> Vileness
Spit landing on faces of love

i stand
>> Nearby
>> Watching
>> Helpless

But think of the alternative

Omen

i feel IT coming

My heart is racing
My bones are shaking
My stomach is churning
My mind is rambling
My adrenaline is soaring

The room is crowded
the dead
our guides
many angels
shoulder to shoulder
tight
They are all waiting here too

Just wish I knew what IT was

Will you leave me now that I have stopped pretending to be
Not me?

Betwixt

L'aube à Minuit

Quand le vent froid souffle à travers mon corps
Je me sent encore le sable froid pousse contre mes pieds,
Je flaire et je vois
la belle nature m'entoure en abîme,
Dans ma main
Je tiens l'âme qu'est en partie du mon âme et je sent
le paix
la plénitude
l'éclairement
Tous des souffles je prends
est plein avec
l'espère
l'amour
l'éternité

Ce vent emporte des messages de tous dès âmes dès
amants sur cette Terre - n'importe quoi quel au loin

Mon esprit divague et je sent l'essence de toi

Pendent la nuit
mon âme chevauche le vent trouvé tienne
et ils dansent le monde vers oubli
J'espère je peux rêver ces quatre ans au loin

Quand je me réveille tu est là encore
couché à côté de moi
dans mes bras,
Je tiens le plus précieux existence que Dieu à crée

Mais puis je réalise que tu manque
mon cœur frappé rapide tant que je cherche et essaie saisir ton esprit traîne
en vain...

La plénitude est mort et l'isolement remplit
l'espace vide maintenant dans mon cœur
Je ne peux plus opérer sans toi

Betwixt

Tous les matins « Petit Aile » remplit
mon esprit
mes pensées
mon âme
«prends quelque chose que tu veux»

Tous mes sens deviennent si intense
La forme de tous les chose sent
pittoresque dans mon esprit...
Les Sons de
gens
places
nature
silence...
L'Odeur de tout le monde...
La Goˆut de vie douce - amère
désireux pour ton nourriture...
Les Sentiments de
joie
peur
melancholie
colère
pensifment
espère
désespoir

Ils entièrement paraître retourner à toi

Tu a ouvert mes yeux et a me donné l'harmonie...

Ces memoirs avec tous les battements
de cœur, sont me aider
vivre, mais ils sans bruit tuer
moi aussi

Toutes les fois que je fixe ton photo
je sent quelque fois
le bonheur complète
tant que mon coeur palpite et saute
au le plus haute degré de l'amour,
un sourire prend à sa change mon visage
L'autre temps mon cœur sombre

Betwixt

Je desire pour ton touche,
ton plénitude...
Mon monde est dedans
tes yeux...
Tu es mon monde
mon amour
- toujours

Dawn to Midnight

When the cold wind blows through my body
I still feel the cold sand pushing against my feet
I smell and I see
the beautiful nature surround me in abyss
In my hand
I hold the soul that is part of my soul and I feel
peace
completeness
enlightenment
All the breaths I take
is full with
hope
love
eternity

This wind carries messages from all souls from all
lovers on this Earth - anything far away

My mind wanders and I feel the essence of you

During the night
my soul rides the wind to find yours
and they dance the world towards oblivion
I hope I can dream these four years away

When I wake up you are there again
lying next to me
in my arms,
I hold the most precious existence that God created
But then I realize that you are missing
my heart beats fast as long as I search and try to grab your lingering spirit
in vain...

Completeness is dead and isolation fills the empty space in my heart
I can no longer function without you

Every morning "Little Wing" fills
my spirit
my thoughts
my soul
"take anything you want"

Betwixt

All my senses become so intense
the shape of all things feels
picturesque in my mind...
The sounds of
people
places
nature
silence

The smell of the entire world...
The bittersweet taste of life
eager for your nourishment...
Feelings of
joy
fear
melancholy
anger
thoughtfulness
hope
despair

They entirely seem to return to you

You opened my eyes and gave me harmony...

These memories with all the beats
of heart, are helping me
live, but they silently kill
me too

Every time I stare at your picture
I sometimes feel
complete happiness
while my heart beats and jumps
to the highest degree of love
a smile changes my face

Other times my heart is dark
I long for your touch,
your fullness
My world is in
your eyes
You are my world
my love
-always

~translated from French to English

L'Automne et Tes Yeux

Je marche avec des arbres
qui donne la vie
à moi
à toi
à notre amour
Je regarde au ciel et je vois
un oiseau noire contre le ciel blanc
Le tape des ailes sont tous des coups de mon cœur qui cri à toi
"Tu es mon amour toujours et j'ai besoin ton battement de
cœur avec mon battement de cœur comme avant"
Je n'ai que « moitié un coeur"
sue ce voyage

Je vois le soleil illumine des
tranchants de nuages
le distance immense entre les deux,
mon amour essayant t'attend

Je marche dans la forêt où
je suis avec des arbres, mes compagnons.
Ils m'encercle avec
des bruns
des rouges
des jaunes
Je vois un feuille briser au loin
de ces branches et tombe
Le vent emporte le feuille très gentil
comme ça oreille arrière en-avant;
je me sent ton touche encore
de ta main
si clos...

Le feuille met sur la terre avec
la douceur
le paix
Je me souviens de tombant
dans tes bras avec plénitude
Je suis perdue d'âne ton essence
je sais la force de ton amour

Betwixt

Je me sent la buée silente sur mon visage chaque
goutte emporte un éclat de joie
ton amour peint l'essence de moi
Dans la brume il y a des évasions
auquelle je court

J'écoute de clochettes et je pense dés anges qui reçoivent leurs ailes

Tu es mon cloche
mon ange
qui vole si haute et tient
la beauté du monde
Ta voix, ta chanson est angélique
ça m'emporte à la plus belle
rêverie de fantaisie
- peut-être la réalité

Mon regards fixe repousse...
Dans les feuille tomber, je vois
tes yeux, plein des
bruns,
rouges
jaunes,
les feuilles,
tes yeux,
sont trempé avec la pluie...
Je vois le melancholie que j'ai causé
Tu pense des « hommes du cirque"
courant autour de moi
Ils sont des fléau qui dis paître
avec un souffle
Maintenant je sais je suis tiennes complètement, toujours...

Autumn and Your Eyes

I walk with trees
which give life
to me
to you
to our love

I look at the sky and I see
a black bird against the white sky
The flaps of the wings are all the beats of my heart crying out to you
"You are my love always and I need your heartbeat
with my heartbeat as before"
I only have "half a heart"
on this journey

I see the sun shining on
sharp clouds
the immense distance between the two
my love is trying to wait for you

I walk in the forest where
I am with the trees, my companions
They surround me with
browns
reds
yellows
I see a leaf break away
from these branches and fall
The wind carries this leaf gently
like hearing back and forth;
I feel your touch again
from your hand
so closed...

The leaf lands on the ground with
sweetness
peace

I remember falling
in your arms with fullness
I am lost in your essence
I know the strength of your love

Betwixt

I feel the silent mist on my face; each drop carries a burst of joy
your love paints the essence of me

In the mist there are escapes
to which I run

I hear bells and think of the angles getting their wings

You are my bell
my angel
who flies so high and holds
the beauty of the world
Your voice, your song is angelic
it takes me to the most beautiful
reverie of fantasy
- maybe reality

My gaze pushes back...
In the falling leaves, I see
your eyes, full of
browns
reds
yellows,
the leaves
your eyes
are soaked with rain...
I see the melancholy that I caused
You think of "Circus Men"
running around me
They are plagues who say feed
with a breath
Now I know I am yours, completely, always...

~Translated from French to English

Every Moment

Your brightening face
Your dancing eyes
Your words so sweet
Resonate in my heart
To lift my spirit
Each encounter
Something grows within

Letting it out is hazardous
These feelings you may not share
Then the meetings become awkward

In this battle
To live a silent fantasy
Or to surrender —
My heart pounds...

A Mixed Drink of Fear And Love

You gave me your heart to take
I left mine with you to keep
The distance that keeps them apart
Does not let IT breathe

Old Bones

They were on a mission
            of exploration
Along the edge of a rocky cliff

They made up stories and built forts
            from old farm machinery and
Scattered piles of rocks

And then the girl slipped
            on the dead leaves
Past her wild playground

A rock came in the way of her hand
            and she hung there
                        dangling
Not understanding she was alive

As she scrambled back up
            her brother warned her
Not to tell mom and dad

Trust

My toes wrap around the
thin, delicate wire
shaking my stance

You have raised the net
to calm my fears
but I do not want to fall at all

Can you give me
the wings
I need to fly

Or do I wait
balancing
with the question
on the tip of
my tongue

Falter

Come
you whispered
and I walked into your shadow
your light danced in my eyes

A storm rose up and i
glared at it with vengeance
in the turning, i lost the ground
and sank into deep waters

You stayed to reach out
and wait
till I can come again

Proposal

When i fall

i want to be picked up and held

as a sparkling diamond in the

palm of your hand

i want to be given the chance to

start again

with no preconceived predictions

on how I will begin

I want to be a part of

Your excitement

Your desires

Your enjoyment of life

Otherwise

how can we meet

again

on the steps leading

to our future together

Uncertain

So innocent a word
used in casual conversations

Then the world turned upside down
all we knew
was not known anymore

Bare shelves
Empty buildings
What will happen next?

Questions in the eyes of our children
unanswered

But we marched
step by step
on roads
on trails
in our hearts

Uncertainty surrounding

But still moving

Lack of

Gliding along
writing
letter after letter
word after word
story emerging

Something is there
hiding
I feel it from a distance
and getting closer
it's fingers of both hands
curved over an invisible wall
waiting to pull itself up and over the wall

Sneaking in
it pushes against me
no one wants to read your
letters   words   stories
not interesting
you will never finish
there is just not enough
just give up

I push back
my wall against its wall
push farther and farther away
so that my fingers of both hands
land on the keyboard
and write
with confidence

Uncloaking

Worked so hard to be invisible
not to be seen
to blend in
to not put anyone out of their way or
change how someone has to do something
because i breathe
i can take care of myself and
not need any help

    Cut off in front
    hit from behind...endlessly
    don't they see me?
    bigger car...
    don't they see me now?

        Head down at desk
        working away
        missing the get-togethers
        don't they see my output?

           nobody notices
           nobody finds me

               i ask and ask and
               nobody listens
               nobody respects
               all that i have asked
               all that i have given

i don't want to be treated like i don't exist....
so why does everyone treat me that way?

                          you allow it
                    you want to be treated that way
             NO!
             ...

            wait

Betwixt

In front of me is a shiny reflection
fuzzy
an outline
slowly defining
slowly coming into focus
suddenly there
a girl in the mirror staring back at me

I was invisible to myself

Now I am there
the cloak has fallen
to my feet and sunk
down into the ground
and up comes my body
standing tall and visible

I see me
everyone sees me
now

Knocked Down, Again

Caught a bubble
rose up
beauty everywhere
kindling of hope
excitement
how far I have come

POP

Free falling
down into the depth
darkness blankets
covering me

I lay there
still
sobbing
back to where
i always land

Rays of Light

At Last

The path that someone walked on
the footsteps left behind;
The tulip someone smelled
The stone someone stumbled on
The breeze someone welcomed
carrying a message of another...

The blindness the sun caused
the dark figure that appeared;
The moment, the connection,
The completeness, the peace,
The comfort, the joy, the love

The open path to be walked on
the pair of footsteps left behind...

To-

How can you not see my Love for you?
I Love you more than the universe can hold
The pressure of my Love makes the world go round
It releases itself through nature
Through this wonderful world my Love comes through

When the birds sing, their melodies cry my Love
the various tunes
the various pitches
the various tones
are the degrees and the different sentiments within my Love
They reach in and stimulate the nerve endings in
your brain and bring you to high ecstasy
Next time you hear birds sing
Listen
let it Enter
you'll find my Love exclaiming in your ears and growing in your body

The wind hits against your body and blows through every fiber
Feel my Love going through you
every element energized by hot or cold
The breeze carries my message
When you hear the breeze through the trees
it is sending a message to your unconscious
whispering or wailing...
Your id would agree
These repressed feelings come through in your
forgettable dreams

Whenever the sun shines it enlightens the earth,
your heart
with my Love
The warm glow seeps in and fires your body with my
ardentLove
making you sweat

The pale moonlight that illuminates the
mystical night
It is light that makes
dreams come true
It floats down and surrounds you

Rays of Light

It hugs against your body, bringing
the depths of my Love

Every time a star twinkles the pulse descends
towards you
It is the beat of my heart that
wraps around yours
There are many stars a'twinkling that are my
Loving eyes gazing upon you

The rain soaks you with my Love
bringing you to the fragrant hot water that
we sink into

The scent of flowers lingering in the air makes my
Love breathable
every breath you take

The strawberries you eat bring a taste like no other
It is filled with the juice of my Love that is
bled from my heart

Imagine touching the clouds and
flying through them
They bring you to feel the sensation of my Love
exciting and tingling your skin

My Love runs through your veins
In every heartbeat my Love
is pumped through you and to all parts of
you

Do not doubt my extreme Love
It is everywhere you
look
everything you
hear
everything you
touch
so energizing that your reflexes draw
your hand away
It is all that you
taste

Rays of Light

my Love is like wine that warms your
stomach
It is all that you
breathe
Feel it!
I Love YOU more...

You,

the archeologist of my soul...

it pours inside my heart
the pounding and pounding
it might explode
but You keep it pumping
not only of Your love
Your soul and spirit too
You not only teach me how to love
but to express it

my heart pumps for You
but it also pumps for the life
that is mine to live

You taught me how to live life for myself
and for God

I want to thank You not only for the life You have given me
but also for existence of my own
to create

Listen to the grass grow
See the clouds dancing in the air
Feel the air bathe you
Taste the sweet drops of pollen
Smell the vines that encircle you

Trees

The lines cut so deep
With wisdom
With power
With life that reaches towards the heavens

Silhouettes against the
blue, grey, pink, purple skies
Tips attract you
pull you in
raise you up

The mighty, the small
preach creation
The smooth, the rough
All is essential
Plunging down
and grasping that which is indispensable

The Sigh

Entering in to fill my cavity
reviving every pore
Filtering out to join together
the instant forever
The breath you took was mine

Power

The green sparkle and flair
pierce through your eyes to
your heart
Taking control, they escort you
to another world of fantasy...

Rapture so unfaltering
you will enter the game
A whirlwind of passion
The teasing of your pleasures
leave your craving for more...

Feeling every sensation, every
lingering touch
Of soft lips and sweet perfume
Defenseless as the beautiful
outline fades into the
morning dew...

Gifts of God

Creation, an extension of Your Love
every drop of rain
on a blade of grass
that glimmers
in the sun
and falls
to the dirt

and we
taught by experience
to Love
Will soon be ready
to join
You
for eternities

in praising
this gift
encourage us
to remember
all that we
sense

Global Peace

One Peace
Turmoil, clutter
anger, hate
the threshold is weakening

I cannot control the world;
blame put on others,
put on myself
does not work

I can control me;
taking responsibility
accepting myself
brings peace within

By not judging and
loving all
Peace stems away from me
So all will be breathing Love

Two Peace
The heart knows truth
When the whisper
pulses through our bodies and
beats on our brains
The warmth swells within us
spreading hope
Making us swoon in pleasure
Sharing this drink
emanates this calm to others
Creating an enduring bond of humanity

Three Peace
Elemental sharing of human touch
replaces judgment
With understanding
Transcending all senses
Filtering through humanity
Compassion breeds
gently
calmly
Soaking up all

Rebirth

Nineteen years
finally awakening
from a nonexistent
slumber

Tossing around
feelings
that were always
unacceptable

Doing actions
that were never
true

Gliding through
the world as a
phantom
that haunts
this dream

A perfect mold
shaped
by their
dogmatic hands

In between
breaths
I was always
there
hidden inside

Waiting
to pounce
out and
master the world

As I wipe the crust
from my eyes
I see freedom
to write
my own story

Lost, To Words

Knowledge he gave
not by dates, facts, or lectures
but by understanding, inquiry

So much value
questioning humanity
our tolerance

Awakening my spirit
opening my frozen eyes
to see what has been left as unseen

Learning about myself
is this teaching
worldly events directly affect me now

He has given an insurmountable quality of living
inspired my heart, my spirit
to write

All this learning lingers at
the tips of my fingers
light surrounds it

A greater light though, shines
it is starting to dissolve
that what he gave

how do I hold on
and not forget
all that he has done for me?

how do I let go
without saying goodbye
to all that he has placed on my mind?

Yet, how can I forget?
the lessons taught
have made their un-diminishing mark

Martyrdom

Death was always the escape
Where I belonged
What I longed for
Every day
Praying
please let me die

Now each moment holds value, intrigue
Learning how to live fully
Accepting the gift
Of universal Love
Praying
please let me teach

Ignition With A Smile

Along comes a certain salvation
The smile of delight
Wrapping around my heart
Like wax
I start to quiver...

Heart Somersaults

Out of nowhere he emerges
Shooting excitement in my direction

I miss my breath as my heart flips
Filling my cavity with heat

My skin tingles as
Enthusiasm jumps out of my limbs

My heart races
As my mind tries to catch it

And my eyes begin to waltz

The Business Woman

The cool air enters her body
Cleansing, as she steps outside
Readying for another night

She finds her table
They know where to find her
Her glasses sparkling in the light

The room buzzes with others
Here she feels comfortable

She knows many
And meets many
Sharing stories

Silence follows one man's gaze
As he watches her in action
And loses count of the puppets
As she moves another player in the game

Her eyes shine
Her face glows
He knows what she is capable of

A chair is pushed back
Scraped against the floor
His feet follow the path of strings

Sitting down
He uses his power
To cut those strings

The woman is taken aback
He smiles
Challenging her

Her heart starts to beat
Not knowing what to do
And her eyes open up to a
New frontier

Song of a Saint

Silence echoes off the hallow wood
as colors crawl along the floor
from the stained window above

A spiritual wave of melody
resonates down the hall
softly spoken and
expands
sitting in the air

This voice carries
a young girl
up to God

She closes her eyes
to enjoy the lingering beauty
of a boy's voice
who's waves gracefully
float through the door

Daydreams

So much time with eyes open
Searching for what lies within

No fairytale can whisper
The depth of beauty that
Exploded in our minds
Each of our hearts growing within the other's

I again close my eyes to stare
My hand touched reality

Cycles

The child grows from its mother
Eyes open to the first light

Taking and giving
Sharing itself

When there is nothing left to give
It passes the body to the Earth

Its energy joining God
Every breath in sync

Creating a whole new cycle

Precious Moments

Feeling the sand between your toes while the sun warms your skin
A stranger smiles at you and you return it
Feeling every beat of loud music
Communicating only with glances
Eating your favorite food
Talking with a friend
Listening to the rain, then running out to get soaked in it
Wearing your most comfortable clothes
Being proud of someone you love
Making a good play in any sport
Sleeping outside and waking up to ultimate peace
Having a snowball fight with friends...and strangers
Meeting a new person
Warming up under many blankets
Talking away the night
People telling you that you look good
Watching a classic movie with friends
Spending a day with your family
Laughing until it hurts
Crying for hours and finally feeling better
Sharing something that has a lot of meaning
Giving to those who really need it
Finding a common love for all
This is all life is...
these Precious Moments

Tree House

The leaves wrap around
Our legs and arms
As we climb the branch
Lowered to the ground

We dig into the bark
To carefully slide over to
The branch wide enough
For our cartwheels

One hand follows the first
As the ground spins by
And our feet find hardness
As we once again are upright

The sun comes through
In pieces
Around the green leaves
As we ascend to a higher level

Soul Reflections

Combien de temps peux-je
    écrite ton nom?
Je vois ton visage sur
    des corps de autres
Je sourirait quand Je te pense
    et de ton beauté

How long can I
    write your name?
I see your face on
    the bodies of others
I smile when I think of you
    and your beauty

True Love

All your life
your deepest dream
has lain in the folds
of your heart

Now it is here
dredged up from the past
and it settles in the palm
of your hand

Its realization is almost beyond reach
anticipating the gentlest breeze to
blow it off into
unseen eternity

But the wonder rests there
watching you stare in silent marvel
There are no words,
only breath

Outpouring

One look pours through
every speck of my eyes
My words liberate the emotions
sheltered in my heart
and it springs in an arc
from my chest to your hand
Your palms accept
taking in my commitment

Peace

It crawls through you...

Come to a settling
a sense of being whole
with those around

An inner balance
giving you power to climb
above the struggle
destroying the shackles of fear

Give your totality
without losing
Finding the niche
within yourself

Ultimate

I take a swing
and look your way
hoping you'll be there

        if you look up
        and make the pass
        the goal will be shared

                my feet may run
                but hands will seek
                the strength of your throw

                to air I take
                to make the grab
                desired by our foe

        I push my legs
        to land a-ground
        throwing to your swing

the line is crossed
the pass complete
causing us to sing

Becoming

Transforming
my love
from emotion
to action
pulling me
to consciousness
of being
and affecting
your gentle
heart

Passengers

Contently alone, I sit and write

along comes an old friend
telling of his adoration

Soon I am joined by another who
edges his way into my conversation

One more perches
wondering if I'd wear his ring

A telegram arrives
bringing promises of happiness from afar

The speed increases
making it impossible to know my destination

Opening a window
liberation breathes into my lungs

and I leap
only to surrender
into your arms

Sustenance

Come to me as the night rolls in
Gently

like a sparrow lifting off of a
naked branch

Then set down facing me
and smile

Heartbeats

As fingertips touch

in pumps the pounding

rushing through my heart

into my brain and

warming my extremities

Our collective beating together

in one rhythm

Sea to Sea

Rushing in from the caress of the lips
vitalizing the white pearls held in suspension
finding its way upward to the encasing of the spirit
electrifying each nerve in anticipation

Swallowing the essence
flooding over all the inner functions
filling the capacities with thorough euphoria
till it seeps through the skin
glistening with your name

Within Your Kiss

Lips converge creating a vacuum
Entering and exploding
Succumbing to the power
Of coming together
Our feet lift off the earth

Hope

It flies high and fast
       soaring through the air
              above me

My eyes glance up and
      watch it pass
         with my feet bolted
           to the ground

Culmination

Drifting away with glimpses of you
reaching out with fingertips
sustaining my cheek
with eyes penetrating into me
            extracting my heart
                  lifting us above the earth

Clouds racing by
mouth open to breathe
sensation

Desensitization

I reach out
       your hands are fists
I hang on
       we walk up and down
              the same path

Your hands soften
       your fingers spread letting the air rush in
Your hands melt into mine
       we walk finding
              a new path

True

Once I looked into his eyes
      and saw the reflection
I knew I would be secure
      for the rest of eternity

When our hands clasped and
      held onto each other
I knew they would never part

The second I felt no judgment
      but acceptance of my full self
I knew I had a best friend
      for life

Tenderness

Instead of your presence, I have a thought
a memory of you
your body wrapped around mine
before parting to sleep

this comfort pervades till dawn
as the eyelid of my heart opens
to see the sparkling light flowing in
surrounding every footstep I place
until I return to your presence

Sundays

You stand boldly way up high
I lay submissively
soaking you in
through every pore

A fierce wind blows
up against my skin
and whispers a hope
that I leap up and
embrace

I am carried away
far from reality
into an abyss

Anticipation

Out of my slumber I heed
Your voice calling my name

My eyes open into yours
My skin tingles awaiting...

Electricity pulses through

The world disappears

A new level of ecstasy
Overwhelms

And I embrace it

Promise

Quiet whispers flow
through and brush up
against my cheeks

tingling sensation   invigorating my bones

Seeds of Suffering

The seeds of suffering are scattered every day
deep within our hearts
Give those seeds light and nourishment
don't let them hide in the dark abyss
darkness will sprout deep decayed roots
that will rot and spread throughout
but kind attention and watering in tears
will transform those seeds into emerging growth
and eventually bloom into beautiful flowers
the delicate scent which will
end suffering

Humble

Bowing
      and glancing up
            at your expansive
                white light
Solid

Willing to subject yourself
      to these horrors
            to learn
               and be a more understanding
Learned
Soul

Serene Snow

White-gray filling my vision
out of this nothing
slowly floats puffs of
fluff

Swaying
twisting in
slow motion
falling and
landing on my
hot
pink tongue

Laying on the soft blanket
of puffs
quiet eases my mind
soft landings of the snow
is the only sound
as joy bubbles raise
all over my body

Falling In Love

Her eyes tentatively look into Mine
Hello
I see You
You are there
You do exist

Water pools in the bottom of Her eyes and
spill over
one tear
at a
time
slowly moving down Her cheeks

A shaky voice utters
"I am here"
and feet feel heavy in the ground

"I am sensitive"
a bouncy ball starts bouncing
around inside
My heart
joy
excitement
authenticity

I am Her
She is Me
the Girl in the mirror smiles

Healing

Dimly
a light glows
deep within the fissure

An understanding
a lesson learned
from the darkness

The glimmer grows
seeping out of the edges
then it bursts out
in radiance

Another lesson
another fissure morphing
leaving behind the dark
glistening now in brilliance

The light coming out
all around
every crack
rays of light

The shell starts to fall away
piece by piece
shattering to the ground
left behind is

bright
white
radiance

Wholeness
Strength
Harmony
Tenderness

A gentle creature

Safe and Sound

To those who are

Lonely
Lost
Overburdened
Forgotten
Rejected
Sad
Unloved
Marginalized

To those who don't believe you can be yourself
and hide away deep inside your soul

To those pretending everyday to fit in

To those exhausted from all of this

And can't go on...

I am here with you

I see you
I feel you
I was you

I love

I intend my practice of self love, healing, and
nurture to reach out in all directions

To come to you as golden specks of light
Landing gently on your heart
Full of love, compassion and peace

To bring you self awareness of your love
And that you are held
Safe and sound

Always

Finding Love

It's ok to be scared
but not scared away

Kind words and thoughts are needed
as you open up

Let calm waters gently rise up
to quench the fear

Exhilaration

Fall back
      and bend over the top
             of a bubble

                  it rises fast
                      carrying me
                           up
                             to air

W
H
O
O
S
H

     I am there
        on top
           full
              exploding
                  emanating

     and it bursts

                Flinging
          me
        up
     even
   further

Wow

My Job In Heaven

Soaring
        free
           feeling fast wind
                racing by
                    as I fly around, bodiless

        puffy white clouds all around

I paint them
              pinks
            lavenders
         a splash of red
         a spot of orange
       yellow illuminating borders

A landscape of colorful clouds
                 to take your breath away
         to touch your soul with
    a flash of heaven

All Is One

The little boy left behind
The little girl who came to shine

The mean
The kind
All is one
All is one

The meek
The strong
The short
The long
The right
The wrong
Every single one
All is one

The soft
The hard
The one without a care
The one on guard
The black
The blue
Follow in
To see true

The owed
The due
What do we have to prove
All is one

I am the sun, stars and moon
I am all
And so are you

I am you
You are me
We are all on this journey

Rest In Peace

Calling out to you
missing you

A subtle shift in atmosphere
I am here
You are loved
This is how I am now

Warm tingling at my heart
a heavy pull in my chest
grounding
solid
foundational
unexplainable peace

Time to Rest

It is time to go
And you know

Heaviness and fear
lay on you

Cut the cord that ties you

The only thing that awaits you is LOVE

Your fight is over
Time to rest

About the Author

Jennifer Mae is a sensitive soul who has been writing poetry for decades as a way to express deep emotions. She hopes to connect with others through emotions and a sense of oneness. Jennifer hopes that these words will bring healing to those that need it. Jennifer is a wife, a mother, a daughter, a sister, and a friend. To explore more, please visit her website: www.thewhisperofdreams.com.